I0211127

Guitar Picking Tunes

BEAUTIFUL AIRS AND BALLADS OF THE BRITISH ISLES

by William Bay

The guitar used for the recording is a Pimentel Southwestern Steel String.

Online Audio

To access the online audio go to:
WWW.MELBAY.COM/WBM37MEB

WILLIAM BAY MUSIC

© 2020 By William Bay. All Rights Reserved.
Distributed by Mel Bay Publications, Inc.

WWW.MELBAY.COM

Preface

I have always loved the beautiful airs and ballads of the British Isles. The frequent use of modal melodies and the alternating major and minor keys are captivating to me. These melodies are perfect for treatment as guitar solos. I selected 19 of my favorite airs and ballads and I added 4 original compositions done in homage to this wonderful genre. The solo *An Drochshaol* refers to the great famine in Ireland during the 1840's where an estimated 1,000,000 people died.

Many of the arrangements are in dropped-D guitar tuning. I find that these pieces work wonderfully well in dropped-D. All of the solos are presented in notation and tablature. A brief note on the online audio. *Fields of Culloden, Irish Prayer* and *My Irish Home* were recorded on a 7-string acoustic guitar so you will hear an occasional low A note. However, I scored all of the solos in this book, including those, for 6-string guitar. I hope you enjoy the mystic beauty of these marvelous airs and ballads.

Willliam Bay

Index

An Drochshaol
The Hard Times

Dropped-D Tuning

William Bay

Adagio ♩ = 88

© 2020 by William Bay. All Rights Reserved.

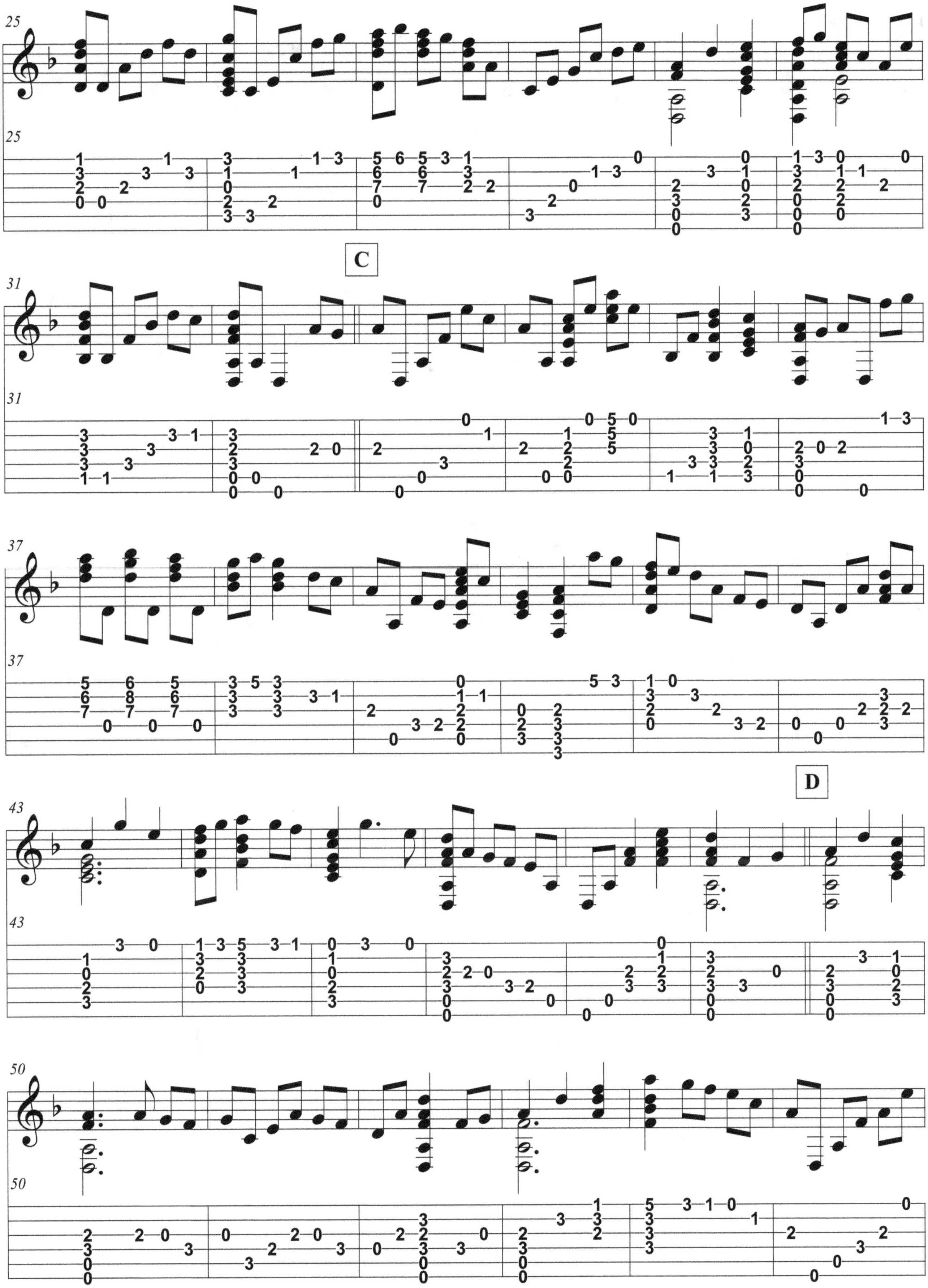
C
D

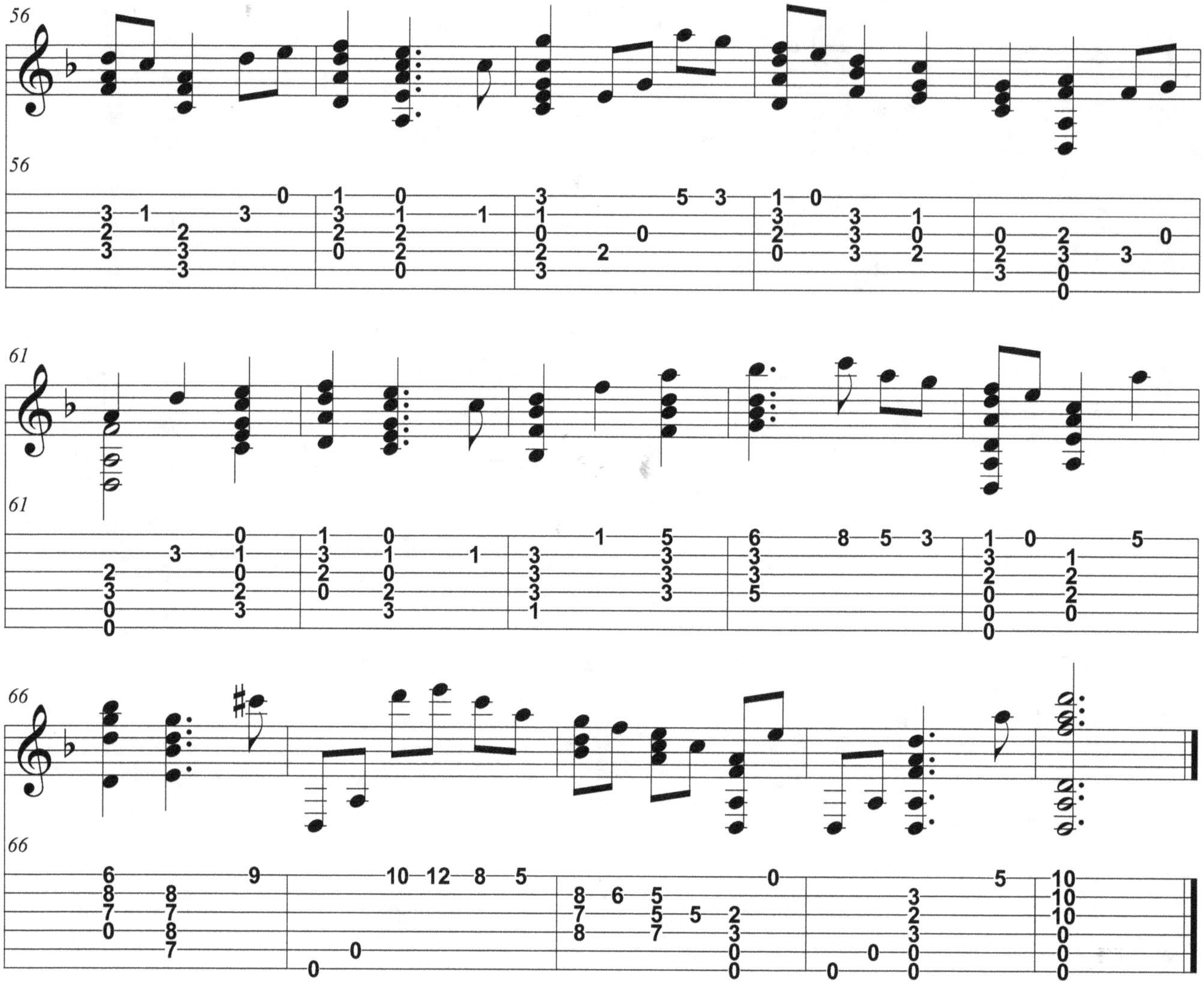
56
61
66

Down by the Sally Gardens

Dropped-D Tuning

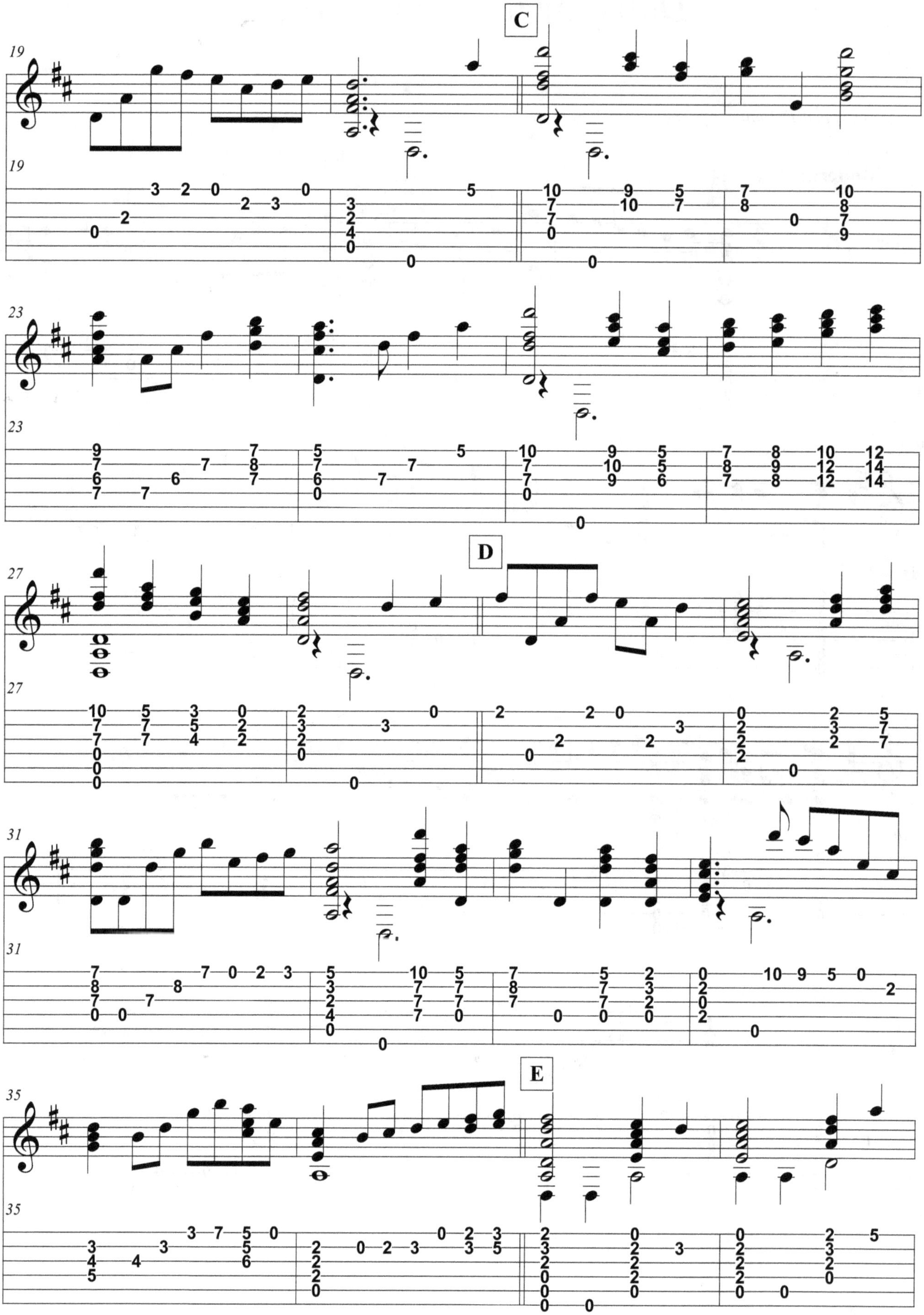
C
19
D
27
31
E
35

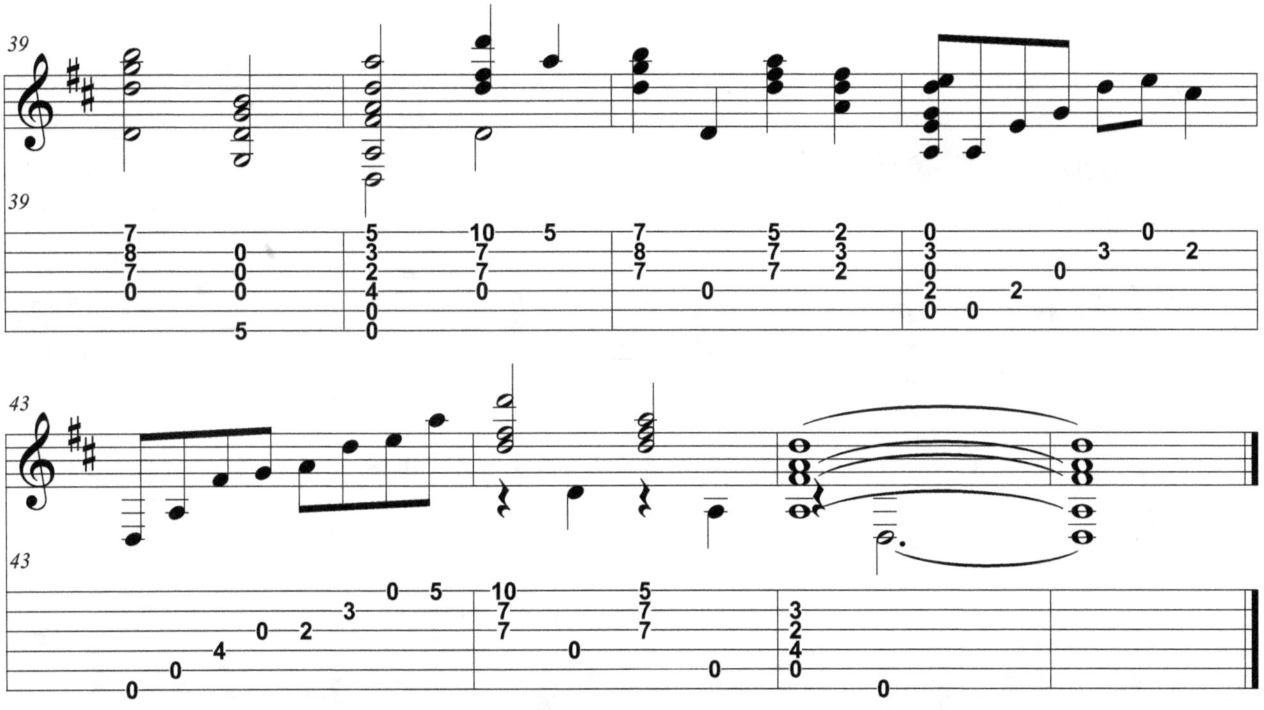
39
43

Believe Me If All Those Endearing Charms

Dropped-D Tuning

Lyrically ♩ = 94

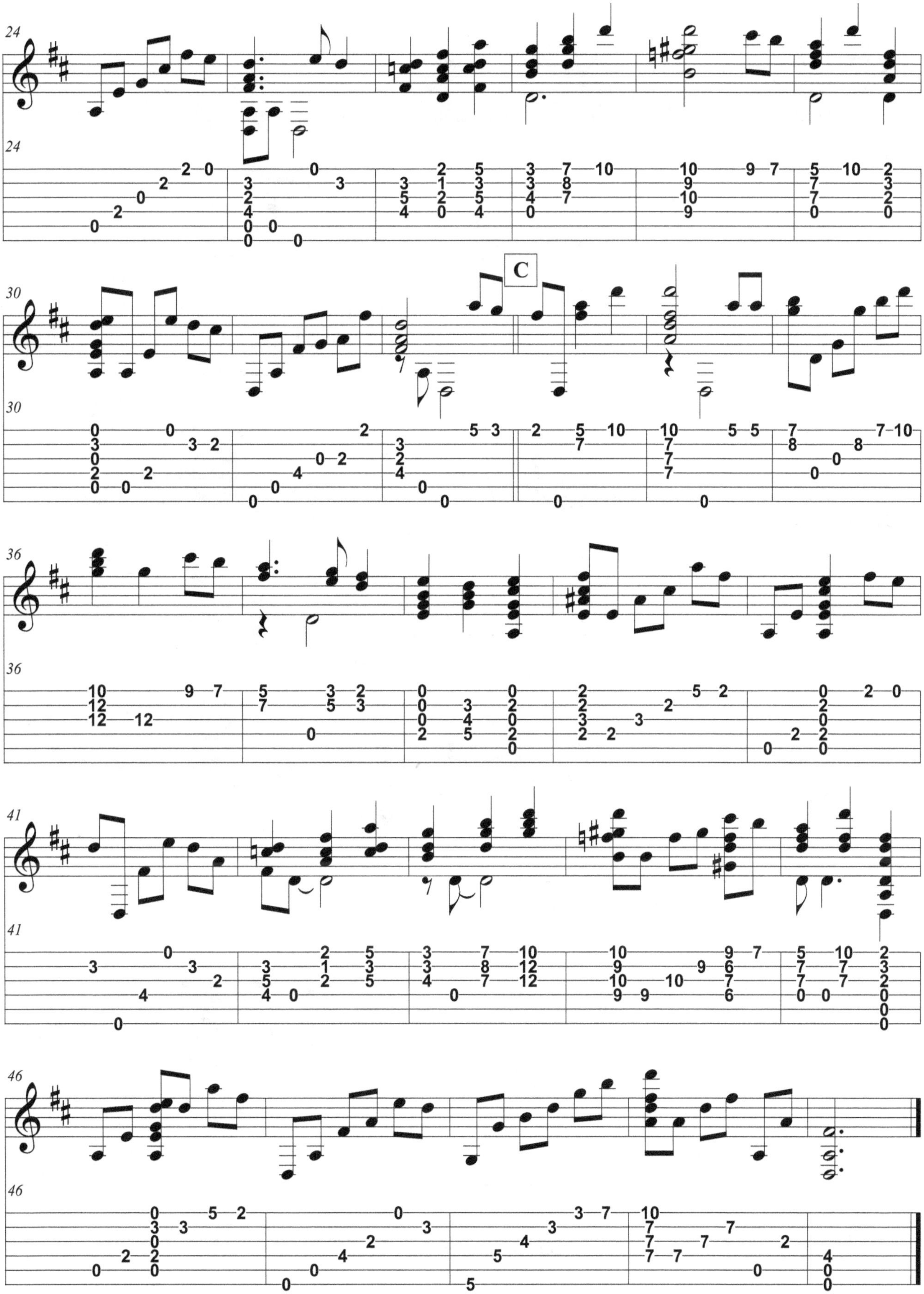
24
24
30
30
C
36
36
41
41
46
46

The Galway Shawl

Dropped-D Tuning

Freely, No set tempo

*On the repeat play the low D up one octave.

Fields of Culloden

Dropped-D Tuning

Lento ♩ = 84

William Bay

© 2020 by William Bay. All Rights Reserved.

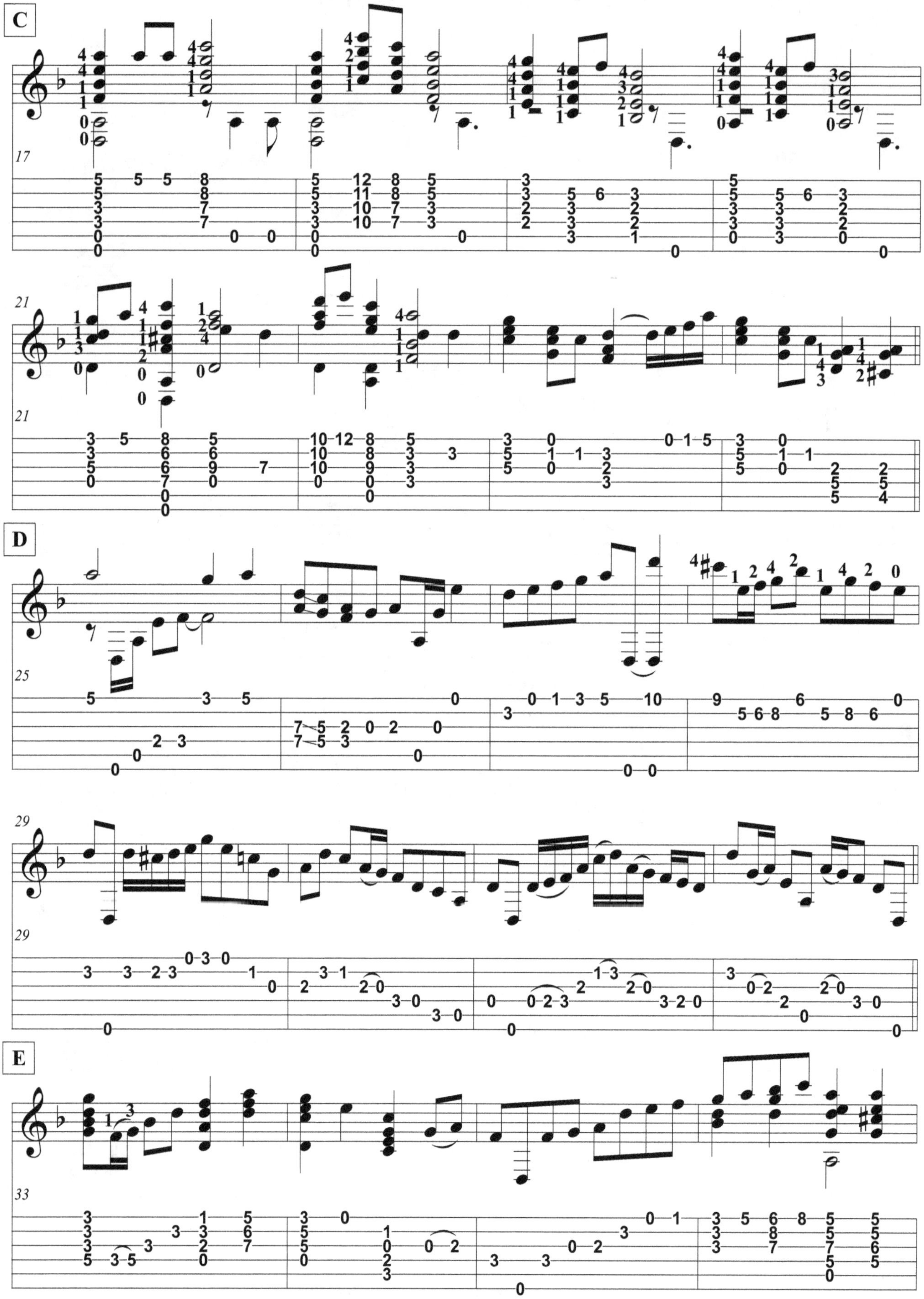
C
17
21
D
25
29
E
33

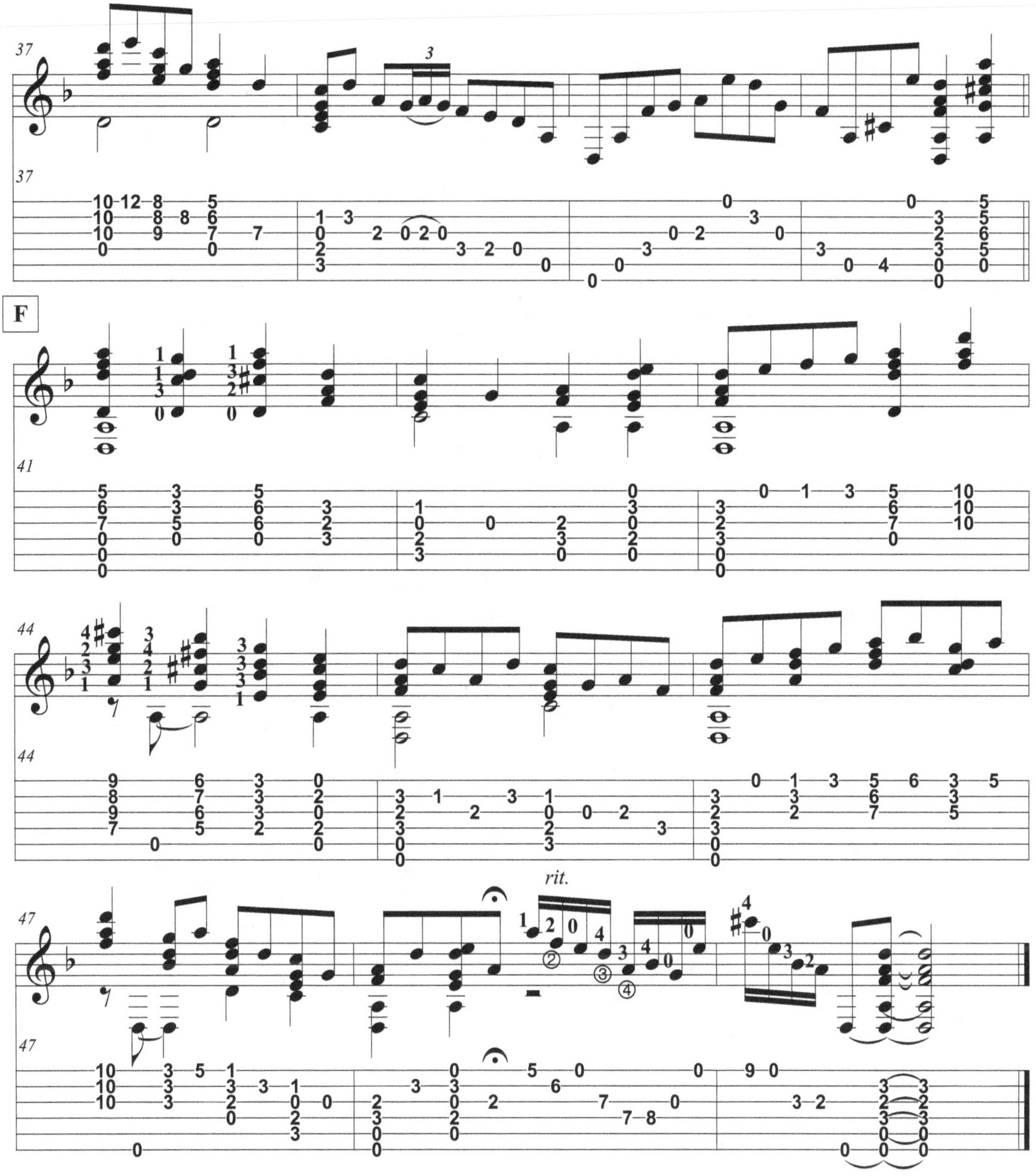
F
rit.

Call the Ewes

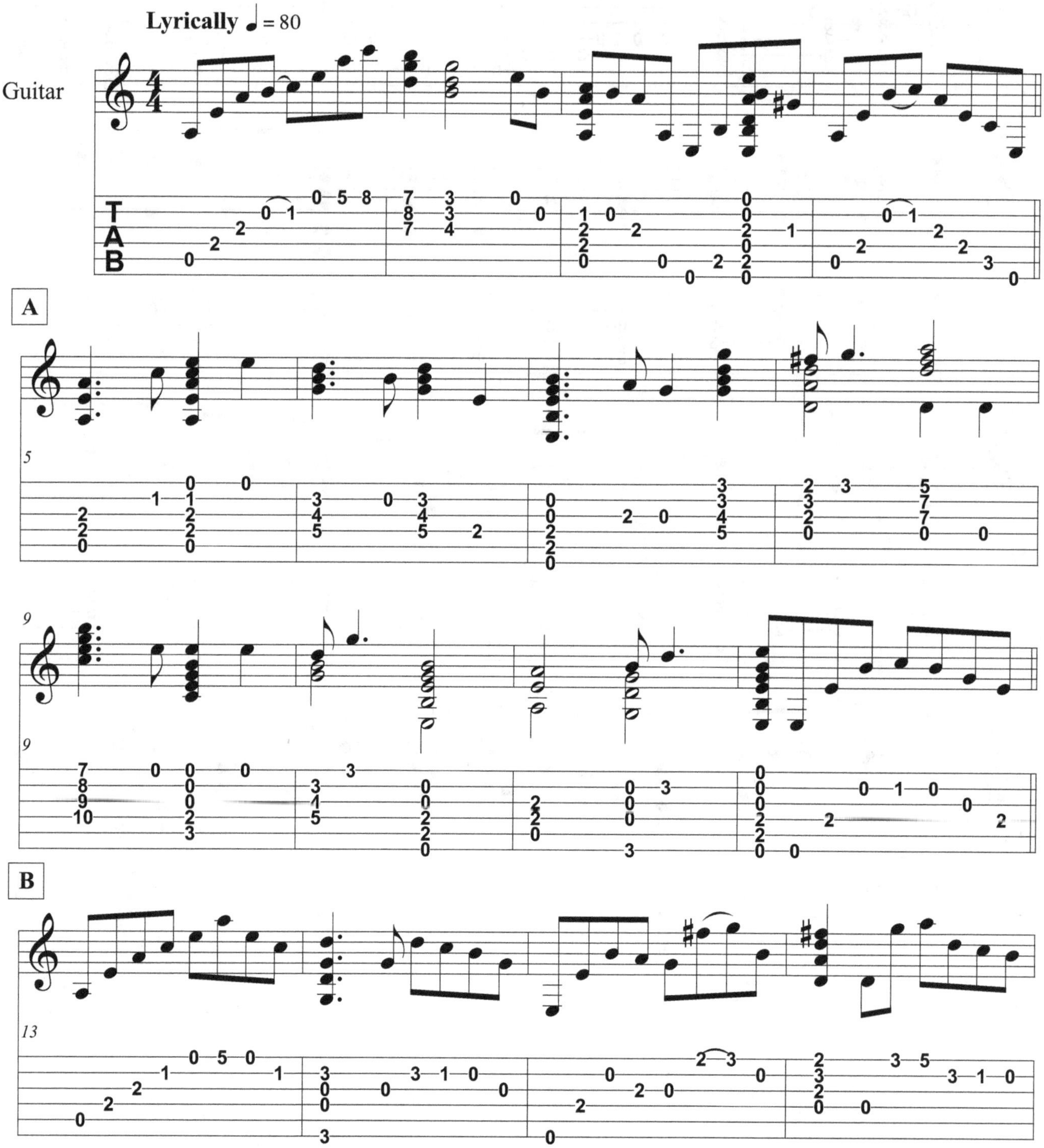

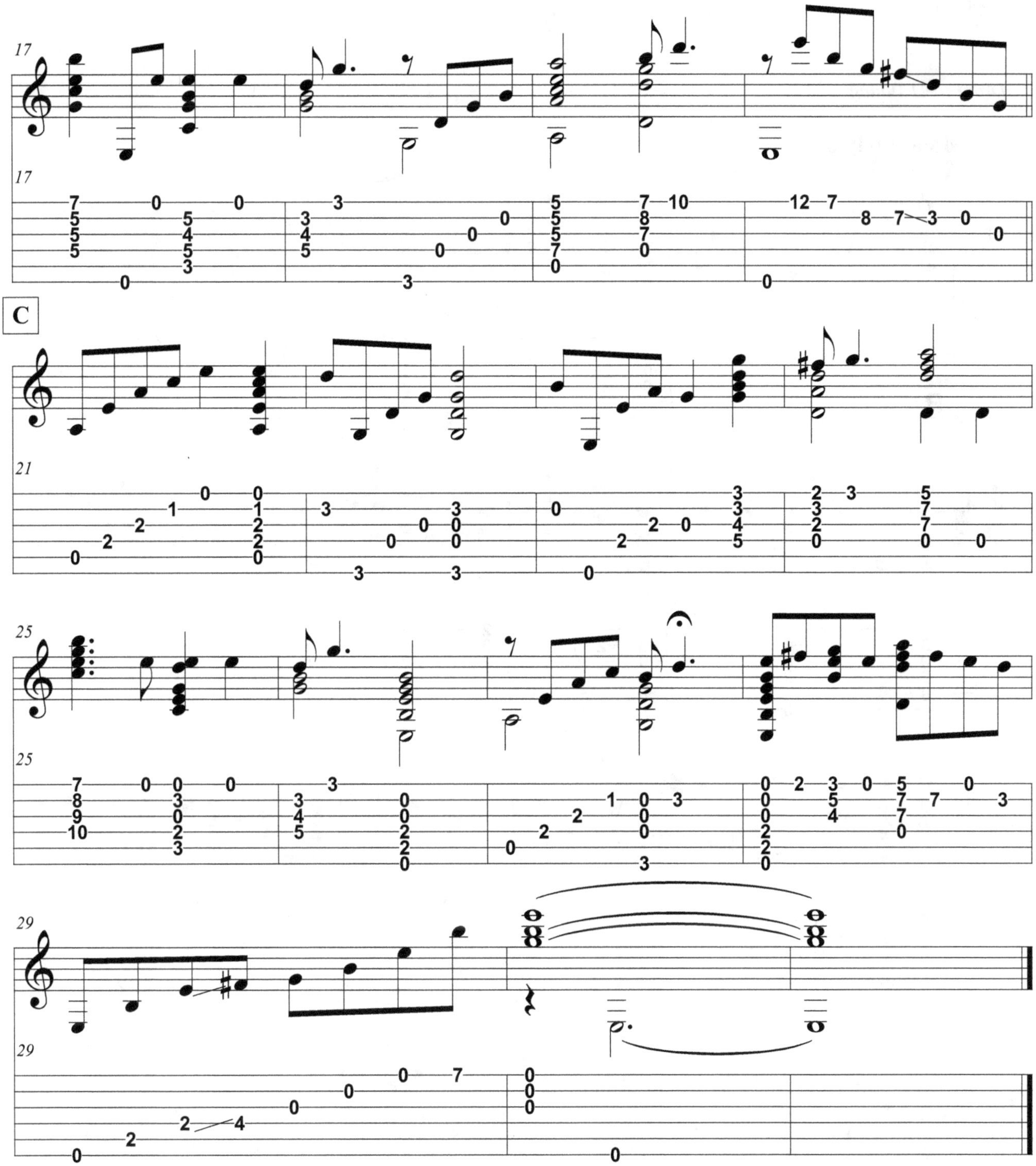
C

Fair Flower of Northumberland

Dropped-D Tuning

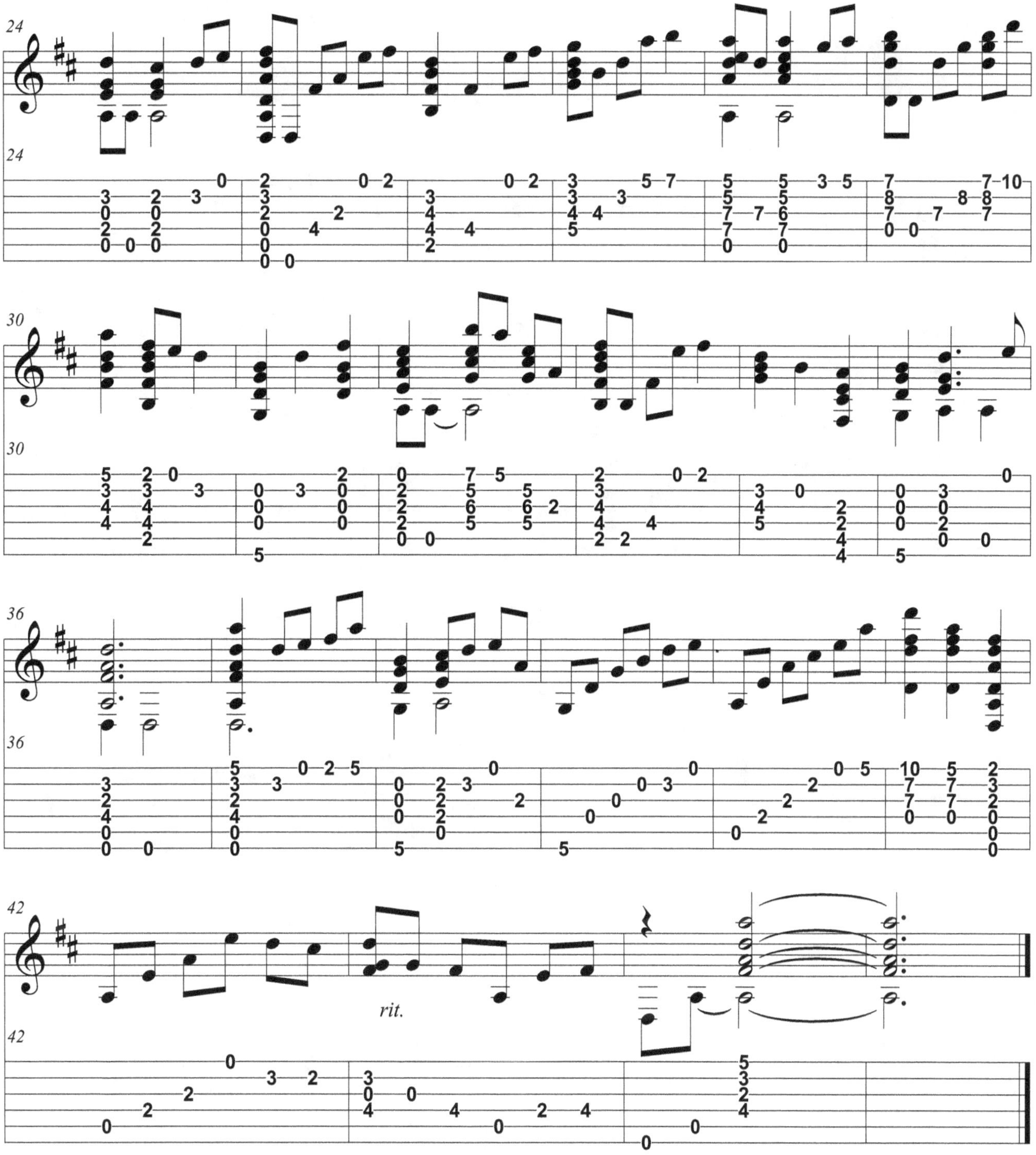
24
30
36
42
rit.

I Went to Visit the Roses

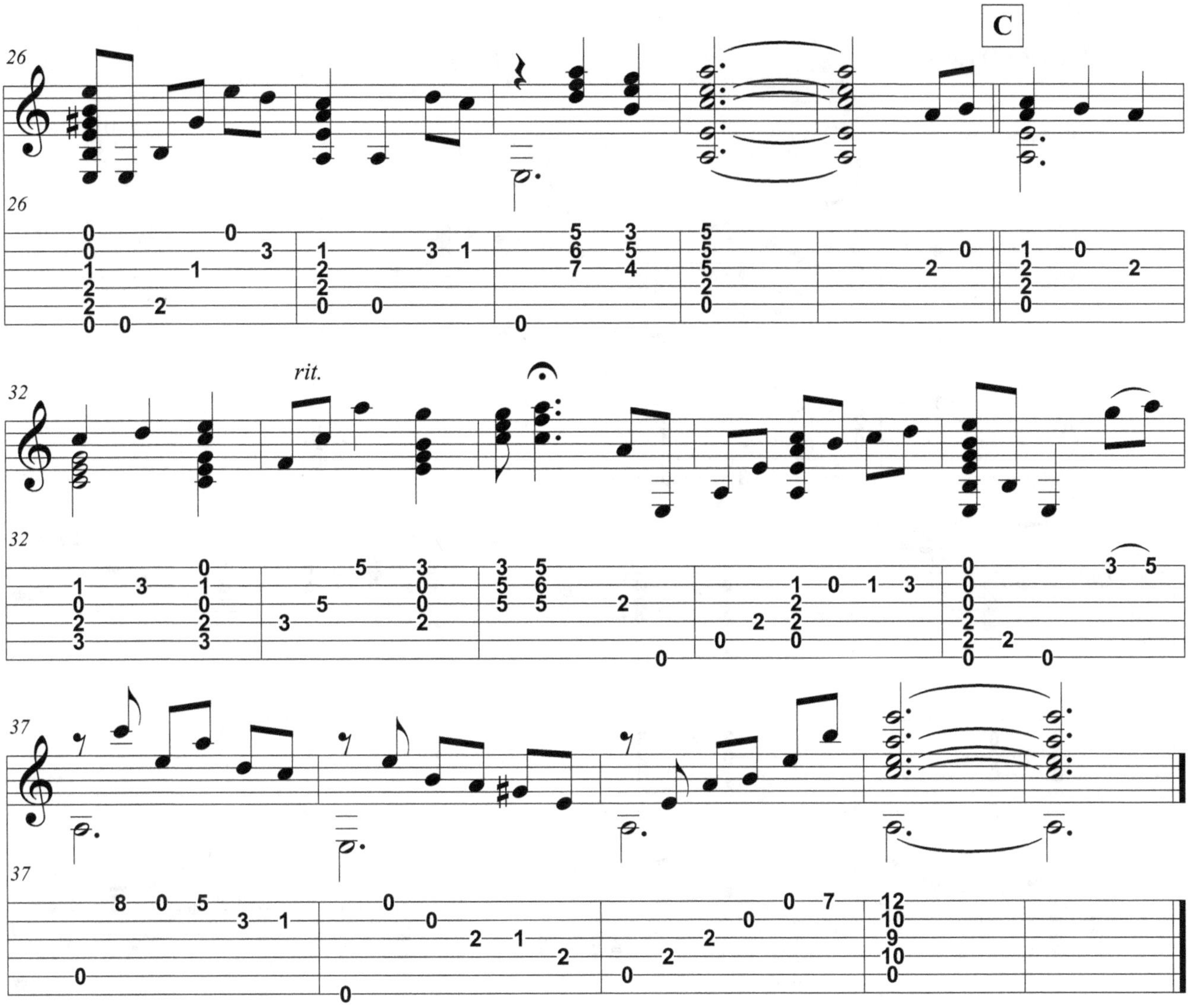
C
rit.

Irish Prayer

Dropped-D Tuning

William Bay

Peacefully ♩ = 80

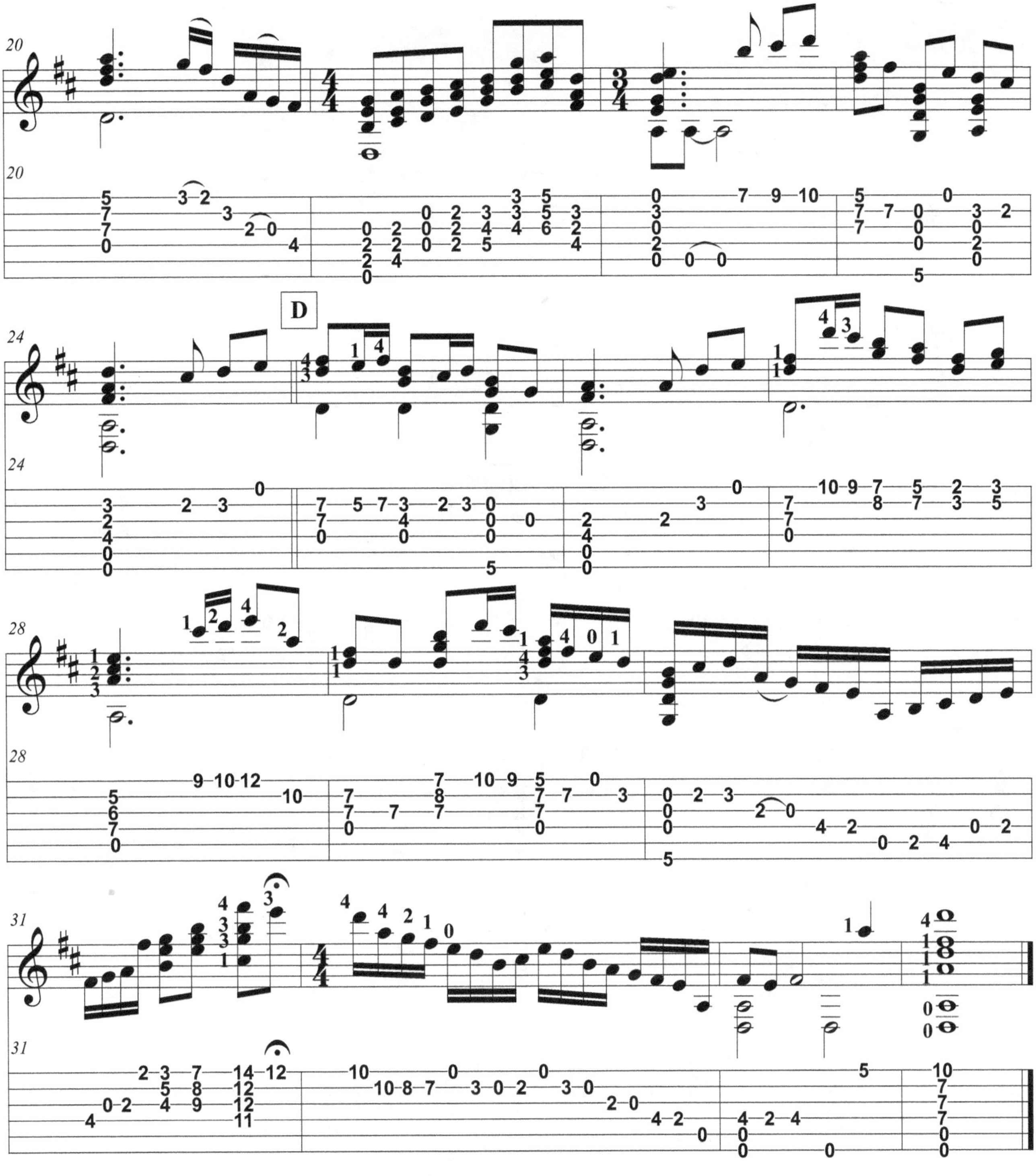
D

Jock O'Hazeldean

Dropped-D Tuning

Slowly and Lyrically ♩ = 80

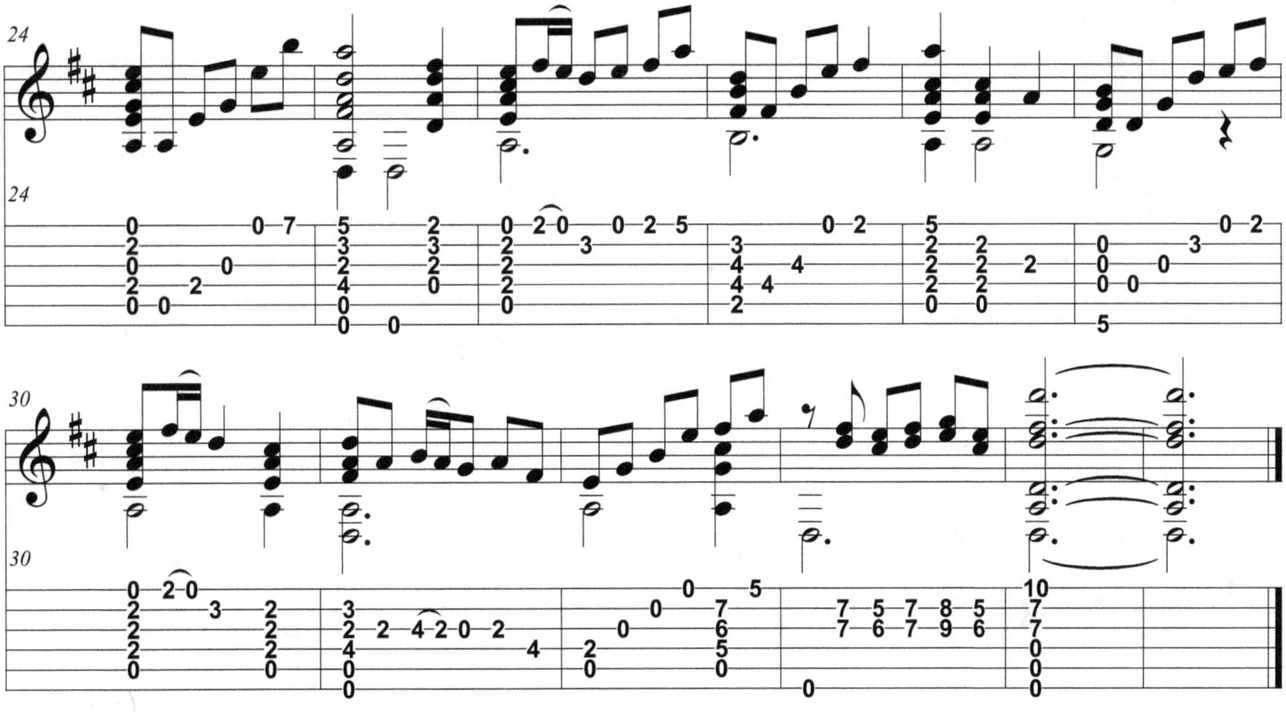

John Anderson, My Jo

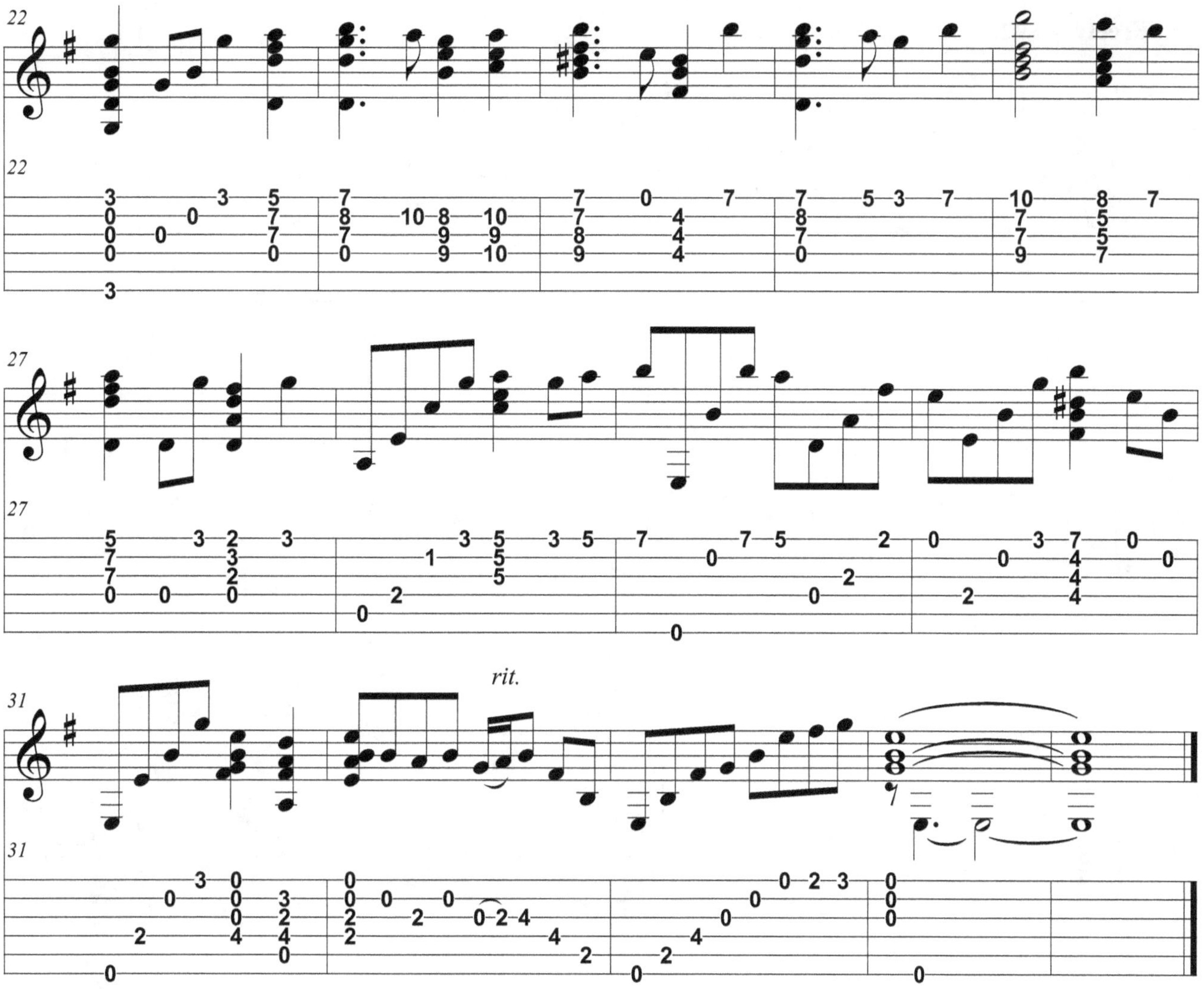
22
22
27
27
rit.
31
31

Cailin Deas Crúite na mBó
Pretty Girl Milking Her Cow

Freely ♩ = 92

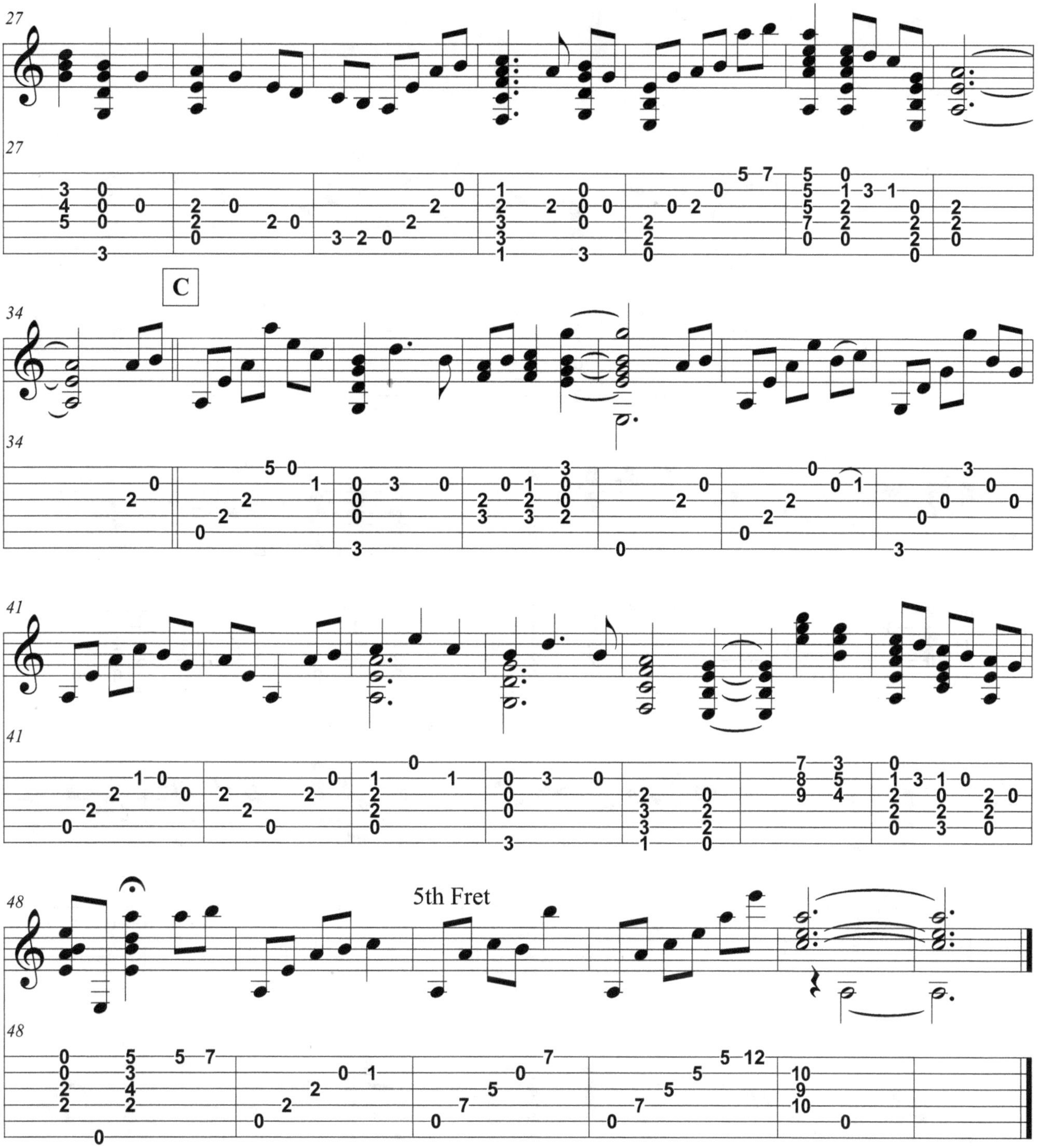
C
5th Fret

Scarborough Fair

Moderato ♩ = 116

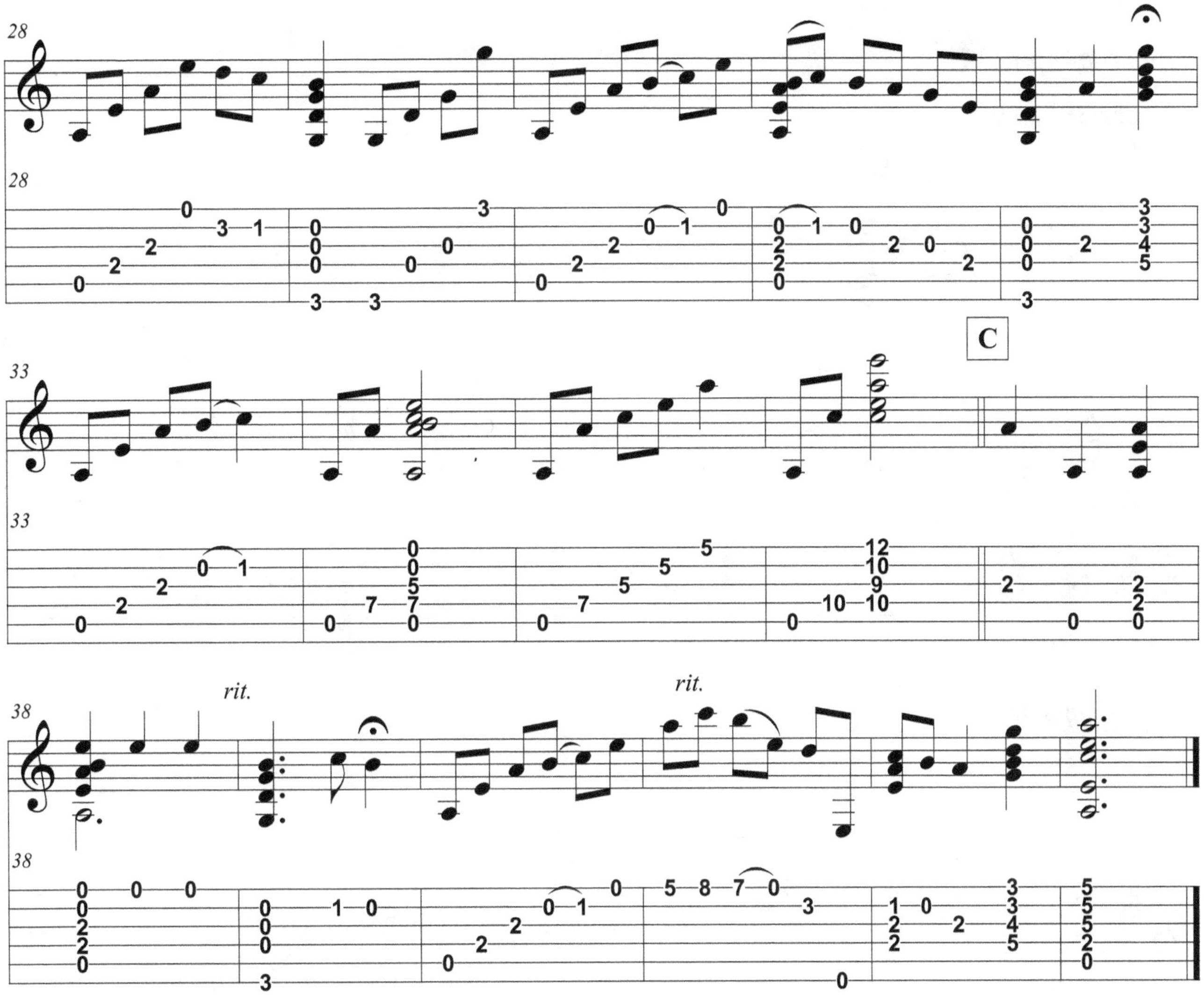
28
28
C
33
33
rit.
rit.
38
38

She Moved Through the Fair

Dropped-D Tuning

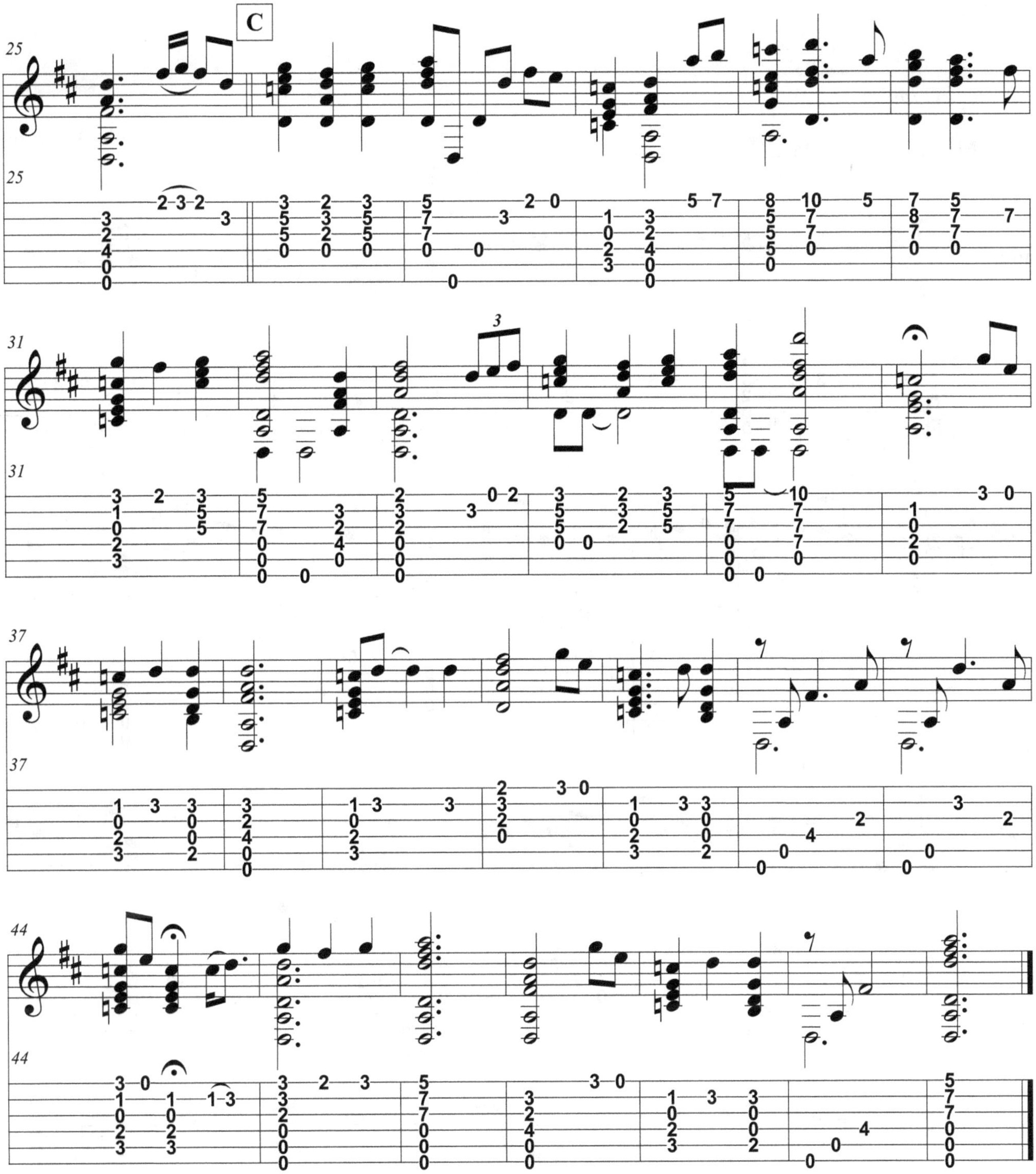
C

Sheebeg and Sheemor

Dropped-D Tuning

Turlough O'Carolan

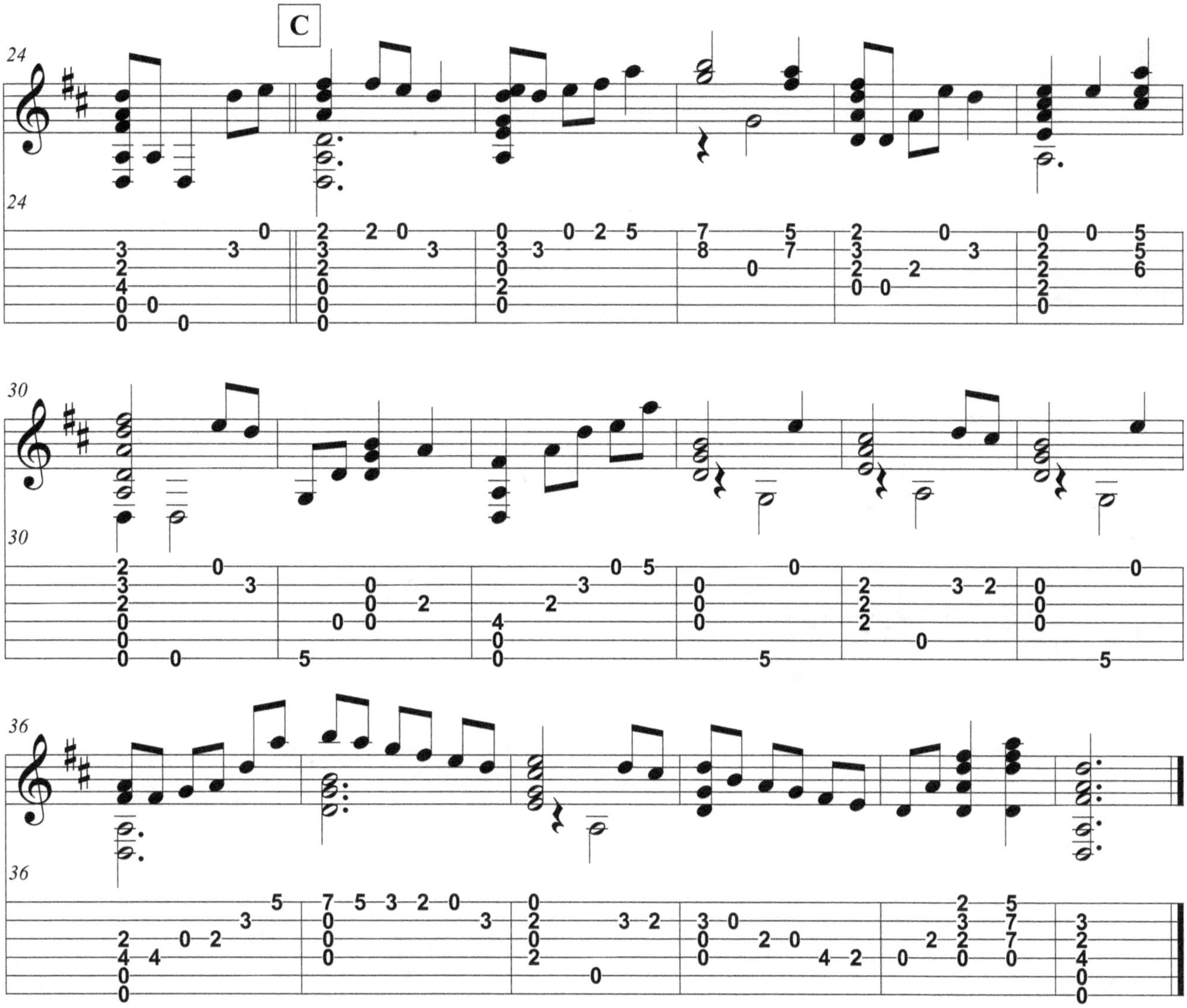
24
C
30
36

Star of the County Down

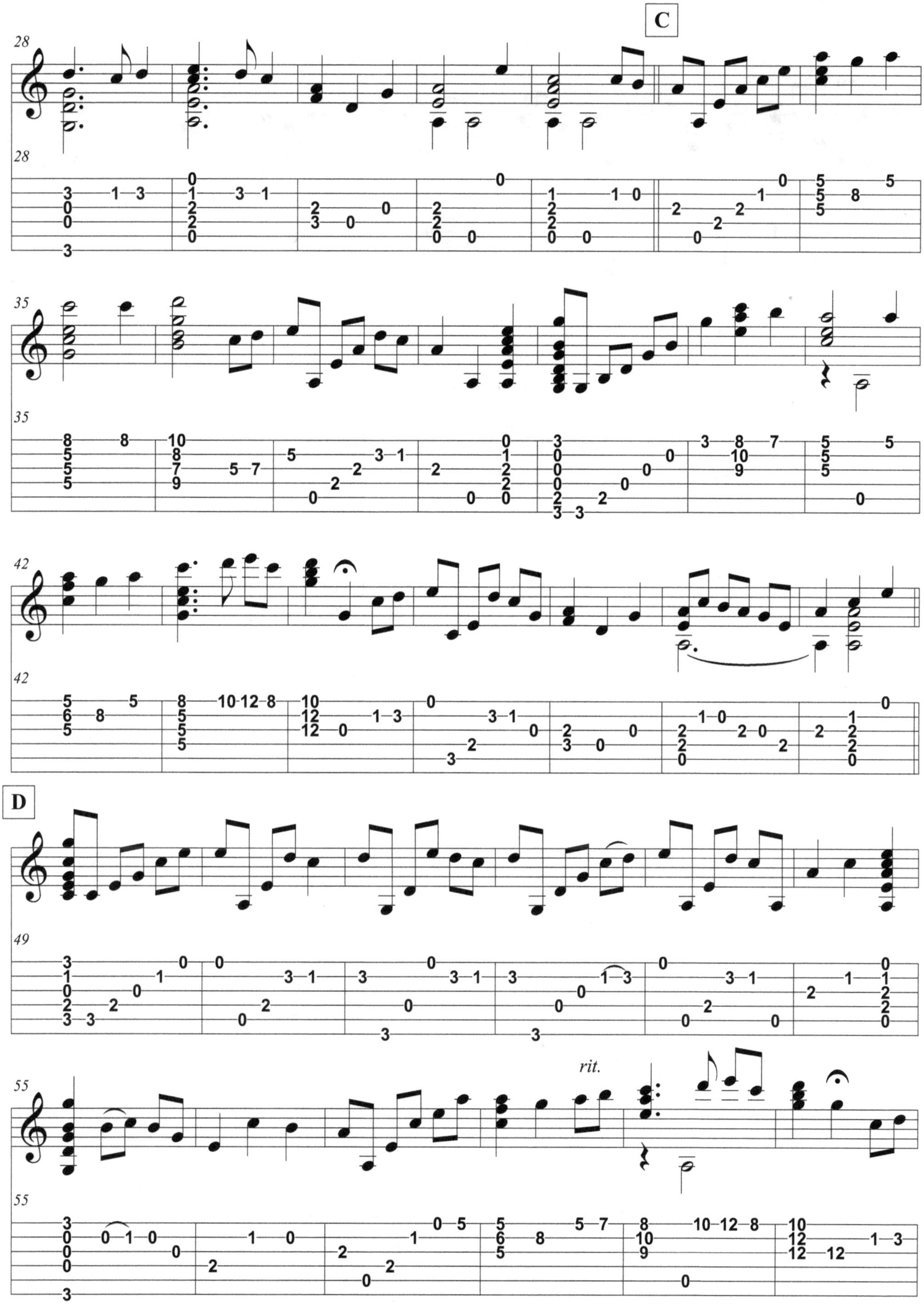
C
D
rit.

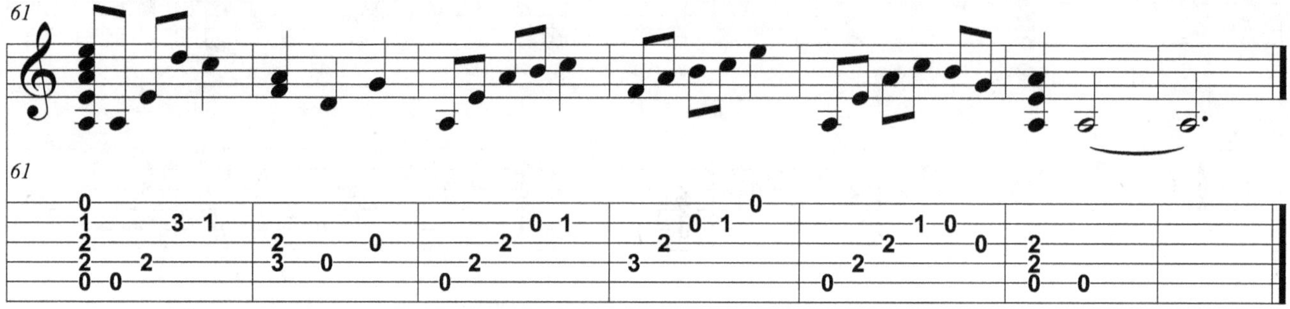
61
61

The Shearing's Not for You

Scottish

Dropped-D Tuning

Andante ♩ = 74

The Flowers of Sweet Erin the Green

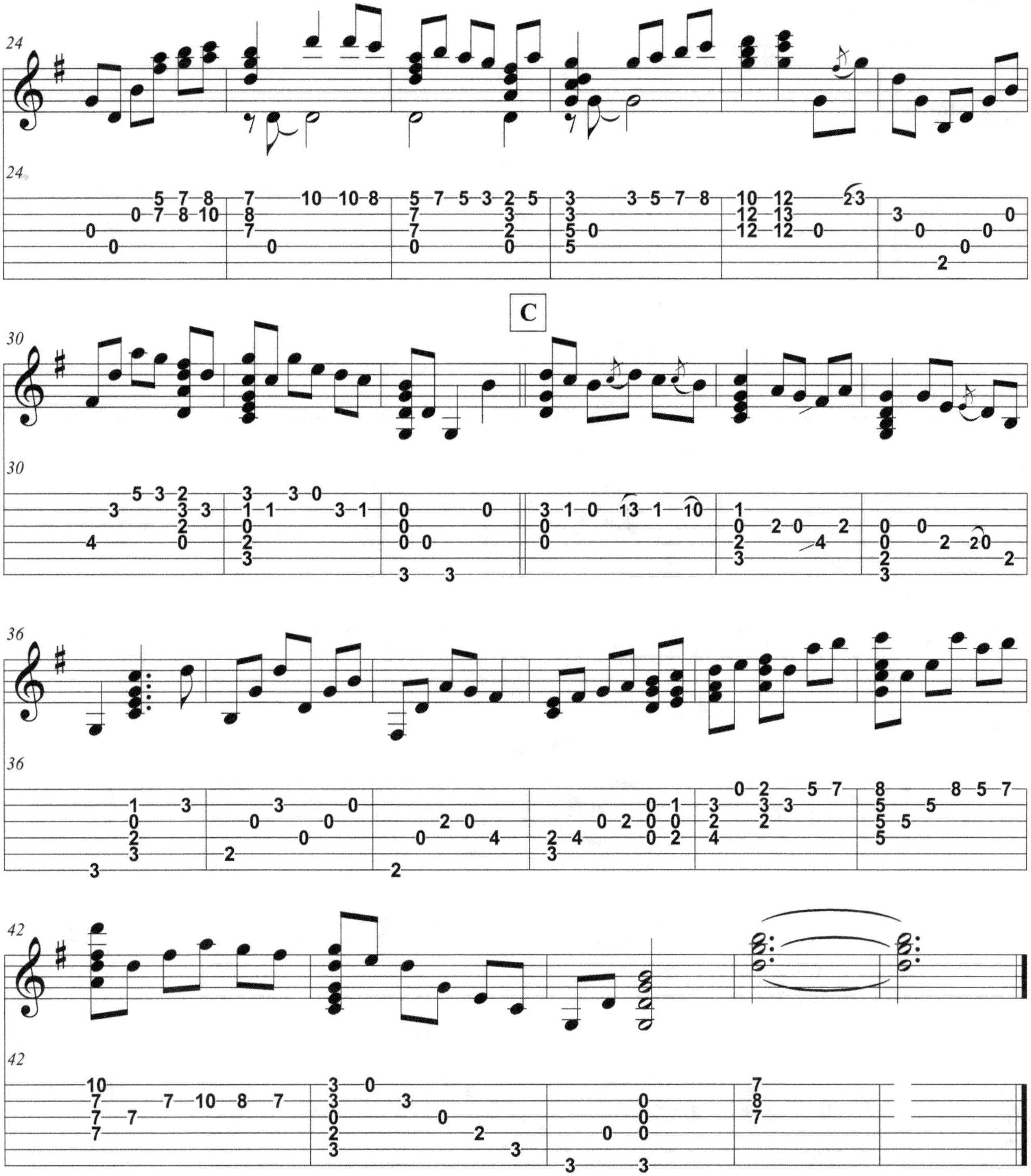
C

The Marsh of Rhuddlan

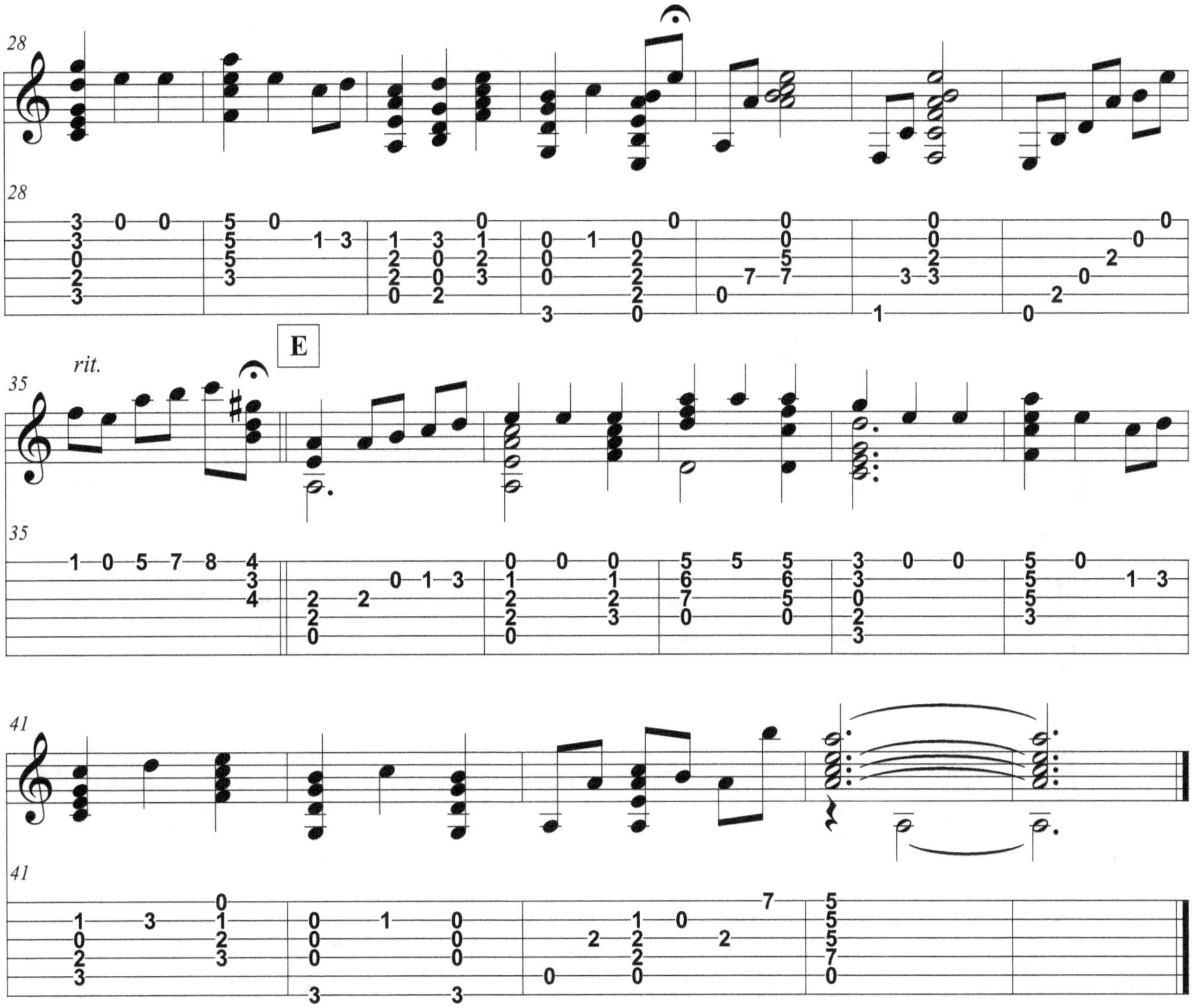
rit.
E

The Water is Wide

Dropped-D Tuning

Lyrically ♩ = 86

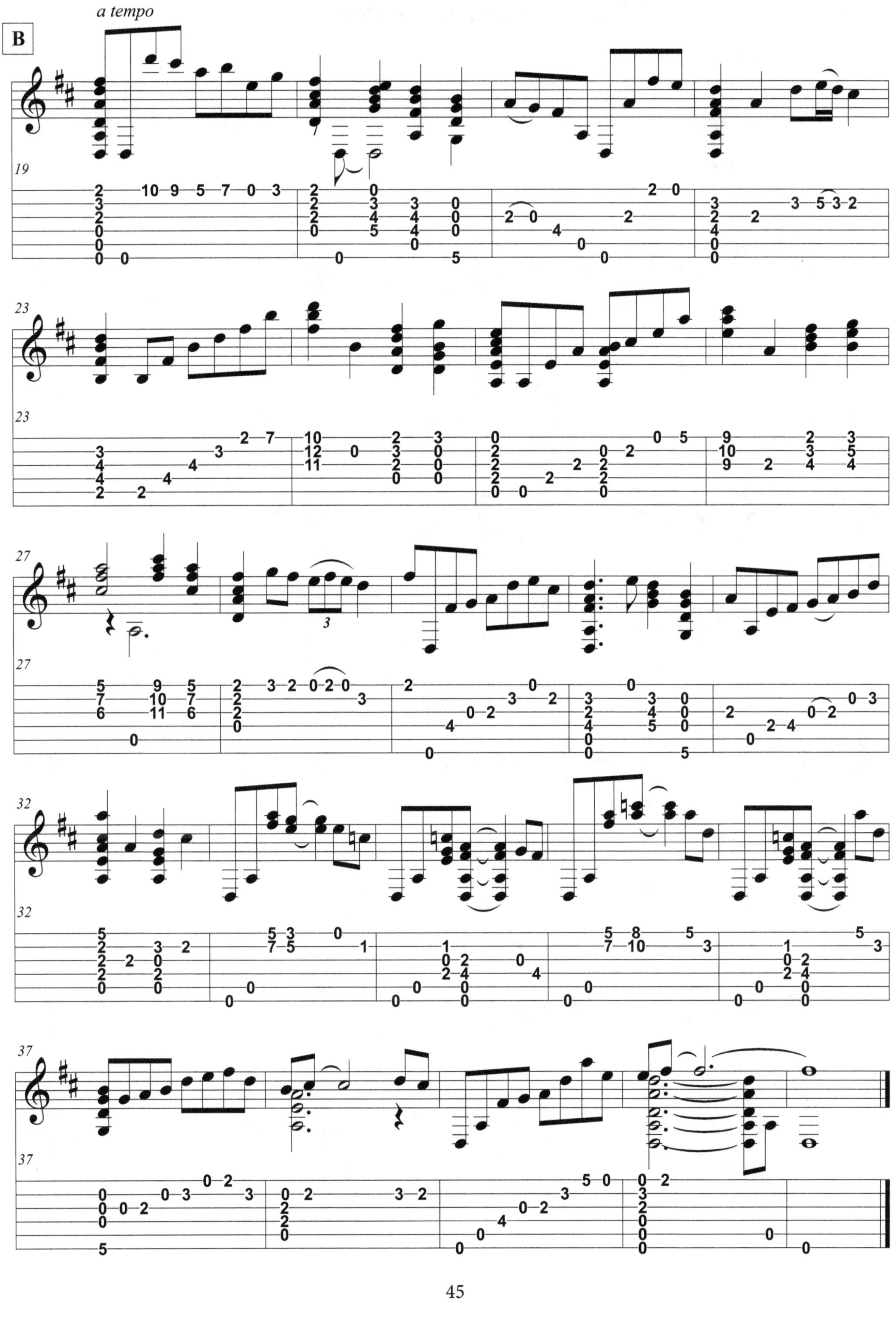
a tempo
B

Once I Had a Sweetheart

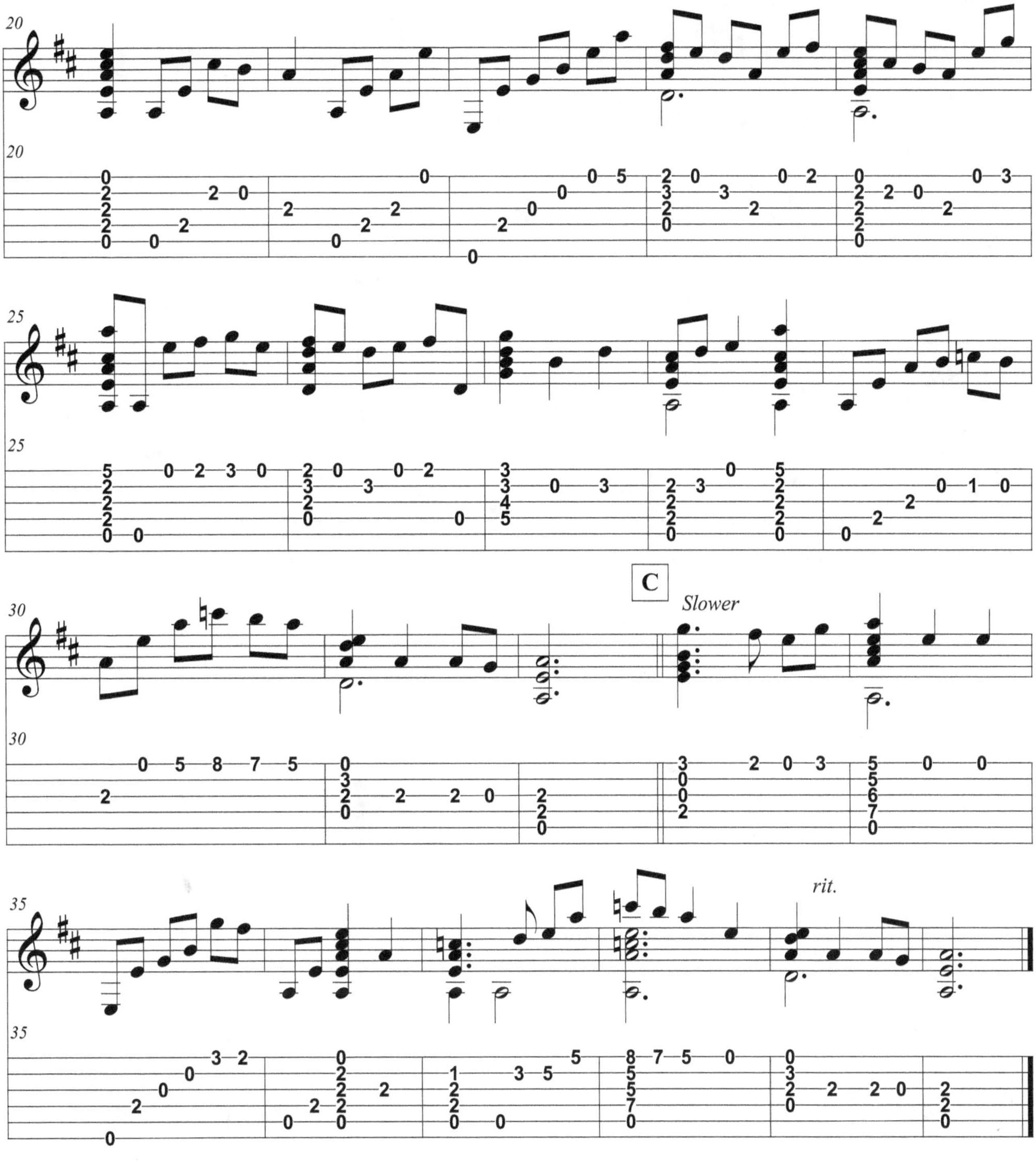
20
25
C
Slower
30
35
rit.

Wild Mountain Thyme

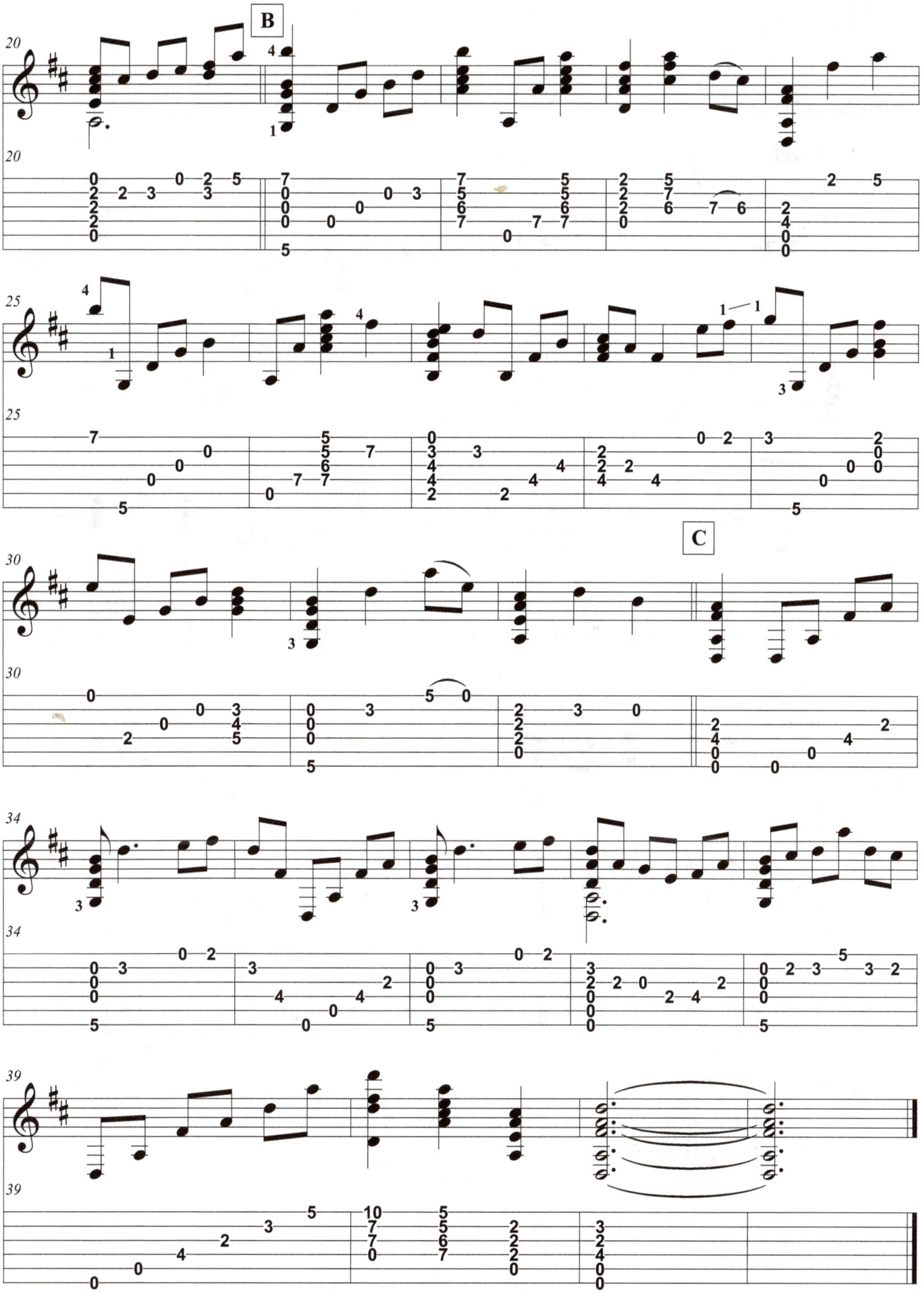
B
C

My Irish Home

Dropped-D Tuning

William Bay

© 2020 by William Bay. All Rights Reserved.

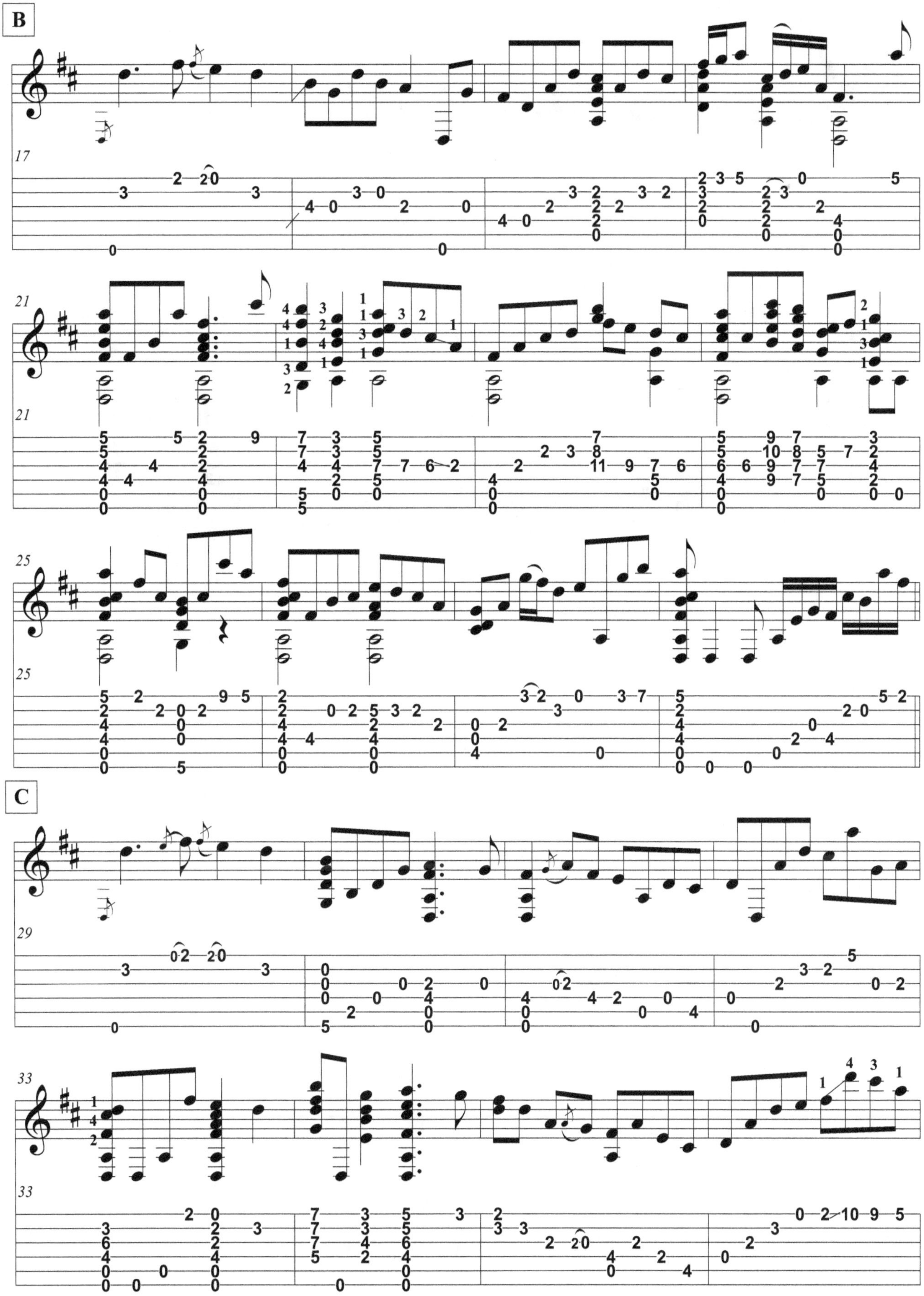
B
C

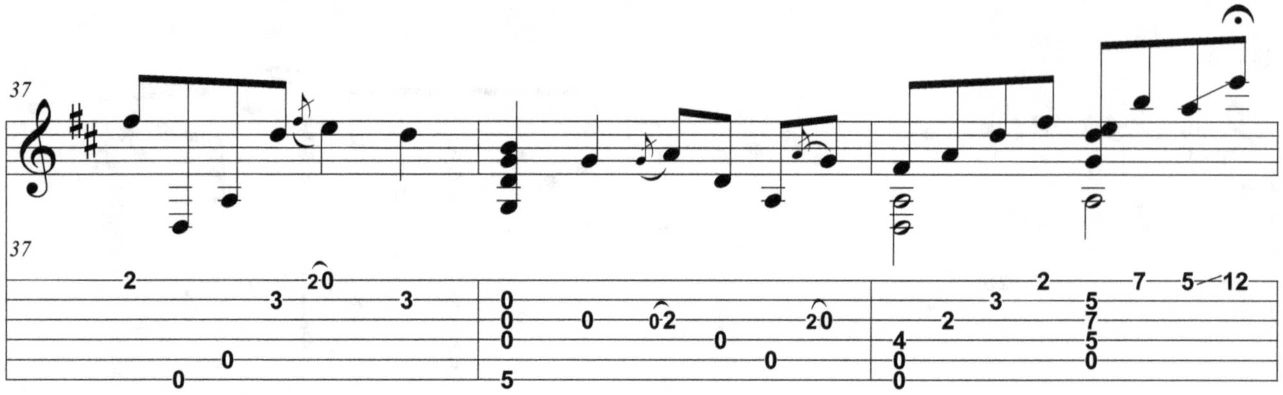
37
37

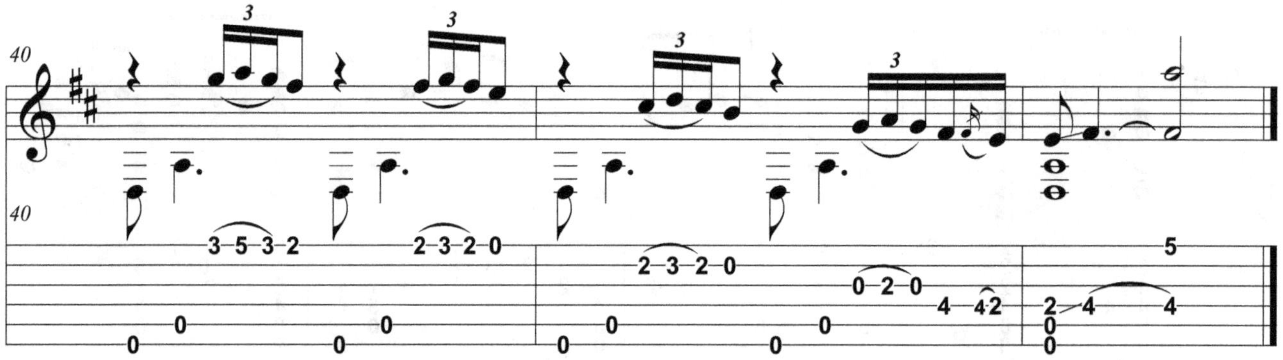
40
40

www.ingramcontent.com/pod-product-compliance
Lightning Source LLC
Chambersburg PA
CBHW080547090426
42734CB00016B/3227

* 9 7 8 1 7 3 3 7 1 6 9 0 1 *